CIVIL DISCOURSE 101

Kreah/Cindy -
you will definitely Relate to
this Book as you Are
very good at conversation.
I pray this Blesses you
As it has me while I
walk it out -
Bless you
Tim

A Conversation Concerning Civil Conversation in America

Civil Discourse 101: A Conversation Concerning Civil Conversation in America

Trilogy Christian Publishers A Wholly Owned Subsidary of Trinity Broadcasting Network

2442 Michelle Drive Tustin, CA 92780

Manufactured in the United States of America

10 9 8 7 6 5 4 3 2 1

Library of Congress Cataloging-in-Publication Data is available.

ISBN: 978-1-63769-778-8

E-ISBN: 978-1-63769-779-5

Dedication

Of all the people that one person comes in contact with during a lifetime, a few of them leave a deep and lasting positive impression. It is to those few in my life that I dedicate this book: to the professional team that I was fortunate enough to work with for years in my first career, to the pastors/teachers/mentors/small group teams that I have learned from, served with and walked with for years, to the teams that built and operated my businesses, and specifically to my wife and daughters, who have patiently and lovingly brought me from being an angry, young rebel in youth, to being a somewhat mature and responsible adult. The impact of those few cannot be over-emphasized.

Table of Contents

Backword

As the title suggests, this writing concerns civility in interactions with other people. Somewhere along the way, many Americans have decided that interaction should consist of forcing their thoughts and opinions on others while viewing others' thoughts and opinions as some sort of an abomination to mankind. Social media has certainly played a part in that process, as it allows people to send messages full of vitriol out to many others at once without having to face the people who receive the messages. And when it comes to politics, some are so intent on forcing their thoughts and opinions on others that they are willing to resort to acts that are far from civil.

In order to address this subject, I found the need to go backward, back to a time when civility mattered to most people. Due to circumstances beyond anyone's control, some of my siblings and I spent nearly three years living with our paternal grandparents. We were quite young at the time, and our grandfather was in retirement age when he started caring for us. One thing he made clear (and we all got quickly) was that young people were to respect their elders and especially the ladies. My father believed the same way, though he was not quite as harsh about it. They made such an impression on me that to this day, I respect not only my elders and ladies, but I am respectful to anyone that will allow me to be so. So much so that I almost believe that the two of them, were they able, would come back from the grave and discipline me in public should I be disrespectful.

A man named Robert Fulghum wrote a book titled *All I Really Need to Know, I Learned in Kindergarten*. I read that book nearly forty years ago and still have my copy. He writes on simple civility: saying "Yes, Ma'am" and "No, Ma'am," "Please" and "Thank You," along with many other acts of civility that people used to learn by kindergarten age. It is an extremely informational book and fits any culture at any age. I highly recommend the reading of that book, especially at this time in our culture, as civility seems to have taken a back seat to argument.

This writing is not done by an accomplished book writer, or by a professor in literature, or by a trained journalist or editor. It is written by a standard-issue, rural American citizen, who happens to enjoy a good conversation, enjoys learning, and enjoys sharing. My high school English teacher would have most likely sent this writing back to me with red marks all over it. (As I was reminded by the daughter of a retired English teacher in my care group, do not end a sentence with a preposition. I had forgotten that particular rule. You may notice others that I have also forgotten. Never mind the grammar; it's just how I speak while writing.) Still, the format of this writing is intended to be a conversation. I realize that it has to be one-sided (I cannot help that), and I would rather have the conversation face-to-face with the reader, though that might not be possible. I wrote this as though I was sharing it with a small group of people, as that is exactly how it came about. I do not pretend to have apprehended and practiced to perfection all of the processes and examples used, as I am learning it as I live it. It was given to me, and I am simply sharing it. I am certain that it was given to me in order to be an example of it. To that end, I continue to study and practice what I've written. The *you* in this missive is assumed to be a Christian, or at minimum, to know and understand Christian beliefs and values. As with anything that the Holy Spirit gives, though, it is useful to all people and to all sides of a conversation.

Being a Christian, I discovered years ago that if I didn't understand something biblical, I could ask questions and learn quickly. To that end, I have asked my pastors many questions over the years. I apply that same process to my Bible study. Any time I read something that I don't understand, I ask God to help me with it. I cannot explain how He helps me, but He always does. As I began to study (and ask questions) concerning the subject of civil discourse, I was led to Jesus as the example. The more I studied it, the more it became obvious as to how masterful Jesus was at the art of conversation!

As I shared it with my small group, we together discovered that Jesus' conversations followed a learnable pattern. That pattern consists of this inescapable truth: The people conversing with Him, whether in a civil manner or in an aggressive manner, could not take Him off of the lesson He was sharing. (Every time He spoke, He was sharing. It was teaching only if the people listening were learning. He simply shared information and whether or not someone learned from it wasn't up to Him. That was totally up to who was listening. That's why He kept saying, "He who has ears to hear, let him hear.")

You see, Christians serve a one-sided God who is in charge of a kingdom that is backward from our normal, physical life. In His kingdom, you have to die to live, give to get, and forgive to be forgiven. That is because He is a one-sided God. That requires explanation:

- God is love (1 John 4:8). He doesn't practice love; He doesn't fall in and out of love; He is love. He loves His created being (you and me) because that is who He is; it's His character. He doesn't love us because we are such good little girls and boys (we aren't). He loves us by choice. He chooses to love us whether or not we love Him! It's a one-sided love affair. And how do I receive His love for me? By loving others, which is also a one-sided affair (John 15:12).

- God is a giving God. He gives because it's who He is. It's His character, His choice. He gives whether we receive it or not. He gave His Son for us. He gave us the Holy Spirit. He gave us grace. He gave us eternal life. He gave us hope. He gave us dominion over all creation. His giving is not dependent upon us receiving it (or believing it). It's a one-sided affair. And how do I receive what He has given me? By giving it

7

away, which is also a one-sided affair (Luke 6:38).

- God is a forgiving God. On the cross some two thousand years ago, He forgave us completely. Our receiving that forgiveness (or believing that He forgave us) wasn't a requirement for His forgiveness. It's a one-sided affair. And how do I receive that forgiveness? By forgiving (Luke 6:37). (How am I going to understand God's forgiveness for me if I don't forgive others?) My forgiving others is also a one-sided affair!

From the simple revelation of these truths came the writing of this missive.

This writing is not intended to be an exhaustive study of civil conversation nor as a guide to all conversation. Rather this is written to connect Jesus' pattern of conversation to those conversations which many of us have either been subjected to already or will soon be. It is hoped that the information shared will benefit our future conversations in some small manner.

The sections in this book are presented in the manner (and order) in which they were given. Each section could be shared as an individual lesson, and each could contain much more information. For purposes of this writing, though, more information is not needed. The reader can easily provide many more examples and relate them to conversations that they have already had in life. The sections are brief, and after the last section and the epilogue, the outline as it was originally given is provided. Any person wishing to share the outline can easily add their own examples.

I speak publicly on a regular basis. Because of that, I find the need to study the material that I share. I would never intentionally mislead someone, either in public speaking or in the course of a civil conversation. Also, I have a small business with several employees. To that end, I am asked questions regularly about current events, or information that someone got from social media, or something that someone has believed in for some time and wants to verify. I attempt to be knowledgeable enough to at least have a decent conversation concerning the information. I do not argue, nor do I allow argument. I can only share what I know, and I have found that many times I learn something new from the simple act of civil conversation. (Also, being in the service business, there are times that customers want to address my team or me in a less than civil manner. That is not allowed in my business. It is a hard and fast rule that the members of the team [including me] are not allowed to argue with a customer. We simply explain to the customer that we will not discuss anything at that level. If the customer can't understand that, then the customer is authorized to have that level of conversation with him or herself outside of the building as they are departing the premises.) We have only a short period of time on this earth to learn. Wasting that time in argument or uncivilized discourse of any kind takes away from that time. I found early in life that the only thing I learned from arguing is that it could be physically painful. (Yes, my mouth got me into more trouble than I could handle more than once, sometimes with a teacher who had no issue with stressing the point with a board across my backside or with someone who was bigger or faster with their fists than me.) I learned that civil discourse is much more conducive to learning and much less stressful.

It would truly be a good thing in America today for people with differing opinions and beliefs to be able to discuss their differences in a civil manner. Regardless of the differences, we are all inhabitants of this planet, and we are going to have to deal with each other. The freedoms that America has held in such high regard should allow for that. Those freedoms should (and must) include civil discourse.

Prologue

Though there has always been aggressive conversation, I have not, in my nearly seven decades on this earth, witnessed the lack of civility in conversation that I am witnessing at the time of the writing of this book. Politicians, who are elected and paid to work with people of differing opinions to properly run our country, are absolutely hostile toward each other. The panels on the news networks that invite guests to be interviewed have members that are absolutely hateful in every way to the guests, who then feel obligated to reply in like fashion. Even family members at family gatherings fall victim to the vitriol and lack of civility. Most movies and television reality shows exacerbate this issue with the "in your face" action laced into nearly every plot or play. It seems to be everywhere.

In my first career as a director of information systems at a regional healthcare facility, I was in charge of a team of people that assisted with the installation of new or upgraded computer systems. Some of those systems affected nearly every department in the facility, and the process would take as much as a full year, depending on the system we were working with. The team was truly a diverse group of individuals from financial wizards to admissions clerks, from clinical techs to medical records transcriptionists; then, there were the technical gurus from my department. What a culture shaker that team was. All of the members of the team were very well qualified, and each had a full understanding of their department's needs. The issue came with trying to get all to understand how their area of the system affected the other areas and how to compromise as needed to ensure that the facility could utilize the expensive system to its fullest. (Keep in mind that the work done during the installation process was added to their normal activities, causing many additional hours of work in order to complete the required tasks.) Then add to that mix the diverse team from the computer company, and for some installations, the consulting firm that was hired to assist with the installation.

There we had three totally different teams, none of which had worked together before and all with their own ideas on how to best utilize the new (or newly upgraded) system for what they needed. And no matter how good the system was, each area needed something more than what was offered. To that end, multiple areas had to build work-arounds to get what they needed, then ensure that their work-around didn't cause issues for other areas. After a while, and after much frustration, members of each team were ready to say things they would not normally say, at least not out loud.

To help keep meetings civil, the IS team introduced a quart-sized canning jar, and the lead IS lady brought it to every meeting. The jar was placed in the center of the meeting table. The rules were simple: If you made a derogatory statement or you criticized another person at the table, it cost you a quarter; no exceptions, put the quarter in the jar and change your approach. This process saved many an argument and/or uncivil conversation. (I must admit that on more than one occasion, I would put a dollar in the jar ahead of time to cover for some of the statements that I knew I would make before the meeting was over, though it did cause me to be less derogatory than I might have been otherwise.) The team had many, many laughs around that jar, and after one difficult system conversion, the jar had well over $300. At the completion of each upgrade or conversion, we would bring all of the teams together for a meal and celebrate our success. At that meeting, we would draw a name, and the person whose name was drawn would be given the jar. That jar would be discussed at length during the meal, allowing everyone on the team to reflect back on the installation process and see how the introduction of a simple process could change everyone's approach to conversation.

America could use that jar right now!

As I look back over my years, I can pick out the people that taught me civil conversation. Some of them weren't aware of their teaching because I learned from watching them. Some that I worked closely with were masters at keeping their conversations civil, regardless of the situation. I envied those people, as my metabolism and my curiosity regularly got me too far ahead of normal conversation, creating unnecessary conversational issues. It took me many years to finally get it. ("Get what?" you might be asking. In an argument, there are no winners. In a conversation, everyone wins, including those that witness the conversation.)

I did not have a book like this one to reference (and I'm not sure I would have read it anyway), so I am glad the Lord put this on my heart at this time. The contents of this book have helped me during the writing, and I pray it be of some help toward civil conversation in America.

OFFENSIVE DEFENSE

"How on earth can you vote for _____?" stated emphatically, with a touch of self-righteous sarcasm. That's how the interaction starts. Not a question, rather a challenge. If you're like most people, your defensive posture comes front and center as you fight off the tendency to want to slap the person right in the mouth. So in place of doing something physical like that, you blurt out some long-forgotten monologue reminding the other person just how stupid they can be by even asking the question. Now, you're on the defensive, and the other person is driving the interchange, which quickly becomes a one-sided affair. As you are speaking it out, your mind is trying to figure out how to get out of this battle of wits without losing your dignity and possibly your teeth. The worst part of this scenario is that while you are in your defensive posture, you are being extremely offensive to the person with whom you are arguing and to anyone else that might be listening. Being offensive is not one of your normal traits and is certainly not a trait you would want to list on your résumé.

By responding to the question or any other question of that nature (which is sometimes intentional on the other person's part) in a defensive posture, you have all but eliminated the format of balanced conversation. Turning that around is extremely difficult, if not impossible.

Most of us have been there, and it is more prevalent in our divided culture today than it has been for some time. All too often, that interaction is with our own family members at a holiday gathering or other family affair. These days, most of these types of conversations are centered around politics, hence the example question above.

In order to address this appropriately, we have to recognize that this type of challenging interaction is not new. It came with fallen man, and there are many historical and biblical examples of these. Though not shared in detail, it is not difficult to gather that the apostle Paul ran into it more than once, as he was beaten publicly multiple times and stoned (left for dead) once. Also, by reading the historical accounts of the post-biblical lives of the disciples, we find that they were not strangers to this type of interaction. It's nothing new.

The person to study concerning this is Jesus. We all know that He was full of grace and truth and that He lived a perfect life (without sin, and we can certainly agree that slapping someone in the mouth because we don't agree with them could be considered a sin). However, He understood something about human beings (remember He created them) that we could learn.

Point: Never allow yourself to be put into a defensive position. The perpetrator of the first part is most likely already prepared for that. You're probably not. In the example we are using, you probably voted for _____ because that person is a better orator and communicator, and at least in your mind, more intelligent than the person you are attempting to converse with. Bringing that into the conversation at that time, though, will only play into the other person's plan. You've probably never felt the need to constantly be prepared for battle when conversing with other (assumed) sane and at least somewhat intelligent people. Because of this, you are ill-prepared for the "in your face" interaction. You becoming defensive turns that interaction into an argument.

By looking at some simple, basic biblical precepts, we find that Jesus knew exactly what He was doing in these types of situations and why:

1. You do not need to defend your beliefs; they are yours. Right or wrong, good or bad, they are yours. You defending your beliefs is most likely not going to change someone else's

beliefs. (Does another person's defense of their belief change yours?)

2. You cannot defend someone else's beliefs. They have their own. At best, you might influence someone else's beliefs, but how can you defend them? They are not yours.

3. You do not need to defend the Word. The Word takes care of itself.

4. You cannot defend God. He's God. As my pastor so eloquently states, "You believing it doesn't make it so. And you not believing it doesn't make it not so." (That might not be good English, but it is a great truth.)

God made man in His image. That includes mind, will, and emotion. (Thank you for that, God. That means that all of us are different, and that is okay.) Your beliefs are wrapped around your mind, will, and emotions. And you cannot change my will, nor I yours. (One of those absolutes that supposedly doesn't exist but absolutely does.) Jesus knew that.

The freedoms that we, as Americans, enjoy today are not found in history books of other parts of the world. To that end, many people don't understand that it has been a long and hard-fought process procuring (and keeping) these freedoms. We are blessed with the freedom of thought, beliefs, and opinion, allowing many to possess an incorrect concept of freedom. It does not mean that you have a right to think, do, and say whatever you want, whenever you want, however you want, and to whomever you want. There are consequences to consider. (As most students above the seventh-grade level should know, there is a scientific fact that exists in creation: For every action, there is an equal and opposite reaction.) Applied to culture or behavior, we find that when your action affects another person in an adverse manner, the reaction that you were expecting may not be the reaction realized. The reality of freedom is this: Your freedom ends where mine begins, and vice versa. Otherwise, it is not freedom. When this concept of freedom is understood, it lessens the need to immediately become defensive.

Jesus did not get defensive in anything He said or did. Even when it meant His life, He called no witnesses and mounted no defense. From His first words to His last, He simply stated the truth and allowed those listening (or not listening) to do with it what they would.

He was a master at turning an interaction into an opportunity to teach. For purposes of this section, it suffices to understand that, by following Jesus' example, we can turn provocation into conversation by not allowing ourselves to be put into an offensive-defensive position.

CIVIL CONVERSATION

One of the unintended and unfortunate outcomes of the social media frenzy in the world today is the pulling away from face-to-face human interaction. In many cases, even the pulling away from vocal communication. To that end, it becomes easy (and convenient) to spout an opinion out across the world without having to deal with most of the consequences that it creates. Everyone can just deal with what I just wrote or said, and if I don't like their response, I just "unfriend" them.

That in itself is bad enough; however, the problem is exacerbated when people are then confronted with having to communicate face to face. If you have not had to deal with the consequences of your statements before, then you are ill-prepared to deal with them face-to-face. In that situation, given the challenge mentioned in the first section, your emotions can very quickly get the best of you.

Emotions are a wonderful gift from God. Emotions allow us to be more passionate about someone or something for which we have feelings. They allow us to bring the world into a more personal experience. They can also cause us to say and do things that we truly regret later and cause damage to relationships that become difficult or impossible to repair. This is especially true in your closest circle of people, your family. (The Bible has much to say on this subject, but that is a topic for another discussion.) Jesus was fully man, so He had emotions. There are several examples of this in the Bible. However, He was a master at removing His emotions from conversation. If our goal is to have a civil conversation with perceived self-righteous, opinionated, arrogant, obnoxious people, then maybe we ought to remove the self-righteous, opinionated, arrogant, and obnoxious attitudes from our side of the conversation like Jesus did.

Point: Ensure that it is a conversation, not an argument. (It's up to you.)

1. Remove your emotions from the conversation. The current PC-driven culture is of the belief that everything is about feelings. Many of the people you will have this challenging interface with have spent their lives honing in on and living by their feelings. Most likely, you haven't. Therefore, if you enter the conversation from an emotional level, it becomes an argument, not a conversation.

2. Ask questions. Then listen to the answers. As hard as it might be to comprehend, you might find that the other person has some knowledge or information that you don't have. (You might actually learn something by conversing. Even conversing with someone you perceive might be mentally challenged. One thing is certain; the other person believes that you might be.) There's an old saying, "Never argue with a fool; people can't tell the difference."

3. Wait your turn to speak. If you're trying to teach someone about conversational civility, it works best if you are civil. (Emotions can most assuredly kill civility.)

4. Speak respectfully. Disagree agreeably. The other person has as much right to their belief and opinion as you do. If your objective is to crush their beliefs, then they can, and most assuredly will make it their objective to crush yours.

5. Use Jesus' example: disarm them with a question or statement, then share some truth with them. What you say to them may not make a lot of difference in their lives, but the truth will speak volumes to the person both during and after the conversation.

Jesus was always respectful, even during His "mock" trial, when the leaders of the culture were lying to and about Him, treating Him with disdain (both mentally and physically) and pushing Him to do or say something that they could use against Him. If He could face death while remaining respectful to other people, surely we can have a conversation with someone with whom we disagree without being disrespectful.

An example of Jesus disarming someone, then sharing truth with them can be found in the gospel of John:

> There was a man of the Pharisees, named Nicodemus, a ruler of the Jews:
>
> The same came to Jesus by night, and said unto him, Rabbi, we know that thou art a teacher come from God: for no man can do these miracles that thou doest, except God be with him.
>
> Jesus answered and said unto him, Verily, verily, I say unto thee, Except a man be born again, he cannot see the kingdom of God.
>
> Nicodemus saith unto him, How can a man be born when he is old? can he enter the second time into his mother's womb, and be born?
>
> Jesus answered, Verily, verily, I say unto thee, Except a man be born of water and of the Spirit, he cannot enter into the kingdom of God.
>
> That which is born of the flesh is flesh; and that which is born of the Spirit is spirit.
>
> Marvel not that I said unto thee, Ye must be born again.
>
> The wind bloweth where it listeth, and thou hearest the sound thereof, but canst not tell whence it cometh, and whither it goeth: so is every one that is born of the Spirit.
>
> Nicodemus answered and said unto him, How can these things be?
>
> John 3:1-9

Nicodemus was looking for a physical answer, one to which he could easily connect. Jesus completely disarmed him by telling him

21

what he needed to know, not what he wanted to know. Then while he was disarmed, Jesus shared major truth with him. Nicodemus most assuredly went home that night with his heart on fire and his head spinning. You will note that Jesus took over the entire conversation. Nicodemus did not interrupt or ask any further questions.   The Nicodemus example did not start from a self-righteous challenge, like that mentioned in the first section. Jesus could handle that too:

> And when he was come into the temple, the chief priests and the elders of the people came unto him as he was teaching, and said, By what authority doest thou these things? and who gave thee this authority? [*Our example of this type of question is: How could you vote for* _____*?*]
>
> And Jesus answered and said unto them, I also will ask you one thing, which if ye tell me, I in like wise will tell you by what authority I do these things.
>
> The baptism of John, whence was it? from heaven, or of men? And they reasoned with themselves, saying, If we shall say, From heaven; he will say unto us, Why did ye not then believe him?
>
> But if we shall say, Of men; we fear the people; for all hold John as a prophet.
>
> And they answered Jesus, and said, We cannot tell. And he said unto them, Neither tell I you by what authority I do these things.
>
> Matthew 21:23-27

Jesus disarmed them completely with a single question. Then, by reading the rest of the chapter, we see Jesus share serious truth with them publicly. He took the conversation from them and skillfully and respectfully turned it into a teaching session for everyone there. He did not try to convince the Pharisees to see it His way. He simply told the truth. What the Pharisees or anyone else that heard the conversation did with it was up to them.

At this point, you may be asking, "What question could I ask that would disarm the other person in our example type situation?" Here are a few thoughts:

1. When does human life begin?

2. If a person moves to America from a country that drives on the left-hand side of the road, on which side of the road would that person drive in America? Why?

3. Is truth a what or a who?

4. Is it okay for a thirty-year-old adult male to have consensual sex with your nine-year-old daughter? (The obvious answer to that is an absolute no, or it better be.) If so, then that person just established that there is a moral line that should not be crossed. Ask then, where should that moral line be drawn, and what standard is used to establish that line?

There are many others, but you get the point. All of these questions allow you to take control of the conversation. The purpose of the conversation should not be to "win the argument" rather to share some truth with the other person. If it is a civil conversation with both sides having input, then both parties can learn something.

Know Show

Knowing (and not just knowing but understanding) the subject matter during a conversation with another person is invaluable in civil discourse. During my time working for a regional medical center, I held a position that was considered a professional position. As a country boy that grew up milking cows, feeding farm animals, growing gardens, and working as a mechanic in my father's service business until my college years, I never really felt that I fit in the professional world. However, I got the privilege of working with some of the most intelligent, balanced professional people that I have ever been around. Those people truly knew and understood their professions and were excellent communicators. It has been many years since we all worked together, but we still meet semi-regularly to have a meal and maintain our relationship. I learned everything I could from those people and am still learning today. One of the major things I learned from my time with them is that people who are studied and knowledgeable in their area of expertise are also studied and knowledgeable in many other areas. As I communicated and conversed with each of them, I could see (and feel) the depth of their knowledge and understanding. I believe that to be a driver of their ability to converse with other people so smoothly and with such civility.

In 2012, my partner in an agriculture equipment business, Tony, came to me with a proposal. He had been spending time with his neighbor, who had a small ranch and was interested in raising cattle again. To that end, he asked me to meet with his neighbor, Walt, and I agreed. Walt came to my office, and we talked for quite some time. Walt is an older, soft-spoken, humorous, intelligent man. As we began conversing, it was obvious how much he knew and understood about ranching and life. It was the most intelligent, interesting, and learning conversation I had experienced in quite some time. I later found that Walt had an education from a very well recognized university and had spent his adult life learning, applying, and teaching holistic management, specifically applied to the management of land while raising and caring for animals. (He has traveled nationwide teaching it and has written several very interesting books concerning the subject.) It has been my honor to work around and with Walt since that time, raising cattle on his ranch. (I have to admit that on more than one occasion, Walt has pulled my ranching card. He has to get tickled each time he watches us move the cattle, work the cattle or load the cattle.) I have grown to truly appreciate Walt's knowledge and understanding of how creation and nature work, and to this day, conversation with him is extremely enjoyable.

When studying Jesus' conversations, it's easy to see that same thing. He knew and understood the subject matter so well that trying to trip Him up fell flat every time. Many of the scholars of that time knew much of what He knew, but they fell short of understanding what they knew. Jesus took advantage of that every time and turned the conflict into conversation and teaching.

The word "know" in the Bible, in many cases, means much more than our normal usage of the word. In the first book of the Bible, we find that Adam knew his wife, Eve (Genesis 4:1), and she bore him a son. In the first book of the New Testament, we find that Joseph married Mary even though she was pregnant and did not know her until after Jesus was born (Matthew 1:24-25). In those cases, the word "know" is a much deeper knowing than just knowing about something. That is how we are supposed to know the Word. The written Word is there for us to read and study; however, by allowing the Holy Spirit to guide our study, we gain revelation knowledge of the Word. By gaining that level of revelation of the Word, we connect to the Living Word (Jesus), who in turn is our only gate (the way) to God (the Father). Jesus, in His final recorded prayer, made it clear that eternal life has nothing to do with time or events: "And this is life eternal, that they might know thee the only true God, and Jesus Christ, whom thou hast sent" (John 17:3).

There is an old saying, "If you want to learn something well, teach it." That saying is true because to teach something, you need to know it well. By teaching the subject matter, it forces you to learn it. On a side note: Public speaking is known to be one of the most frightening experiences for people. The proven manner of overcoming that fear is (1) know your audience and (2) know your subject matter. Jesus was a public speaker, and He knew those two concepts well. Again, He is our example for conversing in a civil manner.

At the time of this writing, the world has instant access to tremendous amounts of information. So much so that some people think that because they can look something up on the internet immediately, they know much more than anyone ever has. Unfortunately, knowledge doesn't work that way. Knowledge comes from study. That is why the Bible clearly states, "Study to shew thyself approved unto God..." (2 Timothy 2:15). This issue is addressed in the first book of the Bible. Adam and Eve chose knowledge over God (Genesis 3:6). That instant knowledge created immediate and long-term issues for not only them but for the rest of humanity. Had they waited and allowed God to show them that same knowledge in a studied and balanced manner, things would have turned out much differently. Studying the Word works the same way. Reading the Word regularly and constantly is proper and correct. Allowing the Holy Spirit to guide you into all truth (John 16:13) opens the door to revelation of the Word and how to apply it to everyday life.

Over the many years of my wife and I being care pastors (leaders of small groups), many people from all walks of life and all levels of biblical understanding crossed our path. The hardest people I have had to deal with have been people that have scripture memorized and can quote scripture better than anyone in the room but lack the revelation of the scripture. Being able to quote scripture is a great thing, but we need to keep in mind that the devil can quote scripture too. It's in the *knowing* how the scripture applies to your life and your faith walk that the studying is all about. For that, we need to invite the Holy Spirit into the study.

If you *know* the Word, it should show in your life and in your conversation. It should be obvious to the person with whom you are conversing prior to the conversation.

Point: Know the Word and be prepared to speak the Word in a studied and balanced manner.

1. Jesus quoted the Word when accosted; we can too.

2. Understand how the Word applies to life and explain how and why.

3. Bible-thumping does not work! Sharing from your heart does.

4. Share a non-combative story or truth from the Bible that will connect with the conversation or as a follow-up to the disarming step mentioned in the "Civil Conversation" section.

The Bible is an extremely interesting book. Many of the stories, in and of themselves, are quite interesting. However, all of the stories point to something else. All connect to the central theme of the entire book, Jesus. By studying and gaining understanding of the Word and how it applies to your own life, the process of sharing without provoking an argument allows for much more civil conversation. An example of a story that everyone can connect to is found in the first three verses of the Bible. Given a few moments to share the truth of those three verses (some of which can be searched on the internet for verification) can change the direction of an entire conversation.

In the first three verses, we find all three manifestations of the Godhead. Verse one, God, the Father. Verse two, the Holy Spirit. And verse three, two different manifestations of Jesus (first as the Word and secondly as the light). We also find in those first three verses the three things from which all of creation is built: space, matter, and energy. (Verse one: the heaven [space] and the earth [matter]. Verse three: light. Light is energy.) We also find the spiritual and the physical aspects of all creation. (Verse one: the heaven [spiritual] and the earth [physical].) Just that information alone can change a conversation completely; however, a disarming question can then be asked that allows you to take charge of the conversation. (e.g., it has been in the past three hundred years that man has determined that all of creation is made up of space, matter, and energy. And that energy comes from light. Who wrote the book of Genesis? Most scholars agree that Moses was the writer. That would have been around three thousand years ago! How would Moses know those things that science has just recently verified?)

Again, our example to follow is Jesus. He was a master at gaining control of the conversation, then using that control to share truth. So much so that people were in awe of His teaching. If we know the Word and can take control of the conversation, we too can use that time to share truth. The secret is in knowing the Word, and that knowing should show.

Position for the Mission

In a college course titled Statistics and Probabilities, one of the assignments from the professor was for the class to split up into groups and take a set of statistics to test different ways of making those same statistics produce different results. It was amazing to see how many different results could be derived from the exact same set of statistics. That was when I learned about weighting and other variables that can be utilized. The same thing can be applied to surveys. Marketing surveys can be and sometimes are designed with the objective in place prior to the survey questions being asked. In those cases, the questions are then worded in such a manner as to achieve the required results. (Is it any wonder that many people aren't swayed by polls?)

How a question is asked or posed makes a major difference in the response. That is why the question that we have been using (from the first section, "Offensive Defense") is presented in the manner in which it was asked. That process is commonly referred to as manipulation. The question is intentionally manipulative, with the intent of getting you to respond in the manner in which that person is prepared to attack or defend. If you respond in that expected manner, you have automatically placed yourself into a defensive position and allowed your emotions to override common courtesy and common sense. We have also seen in the previous sections that we can bypass that manipulation by following Jesus' example.

One of the main reasons that Jesus would not allow himself to be manipulated into an emotional-based argument was that He knew His mission. His objective. Not only did He know His mission, He never veered from it.

Our emotions and our competitive training push us toward the wrong outcome. When our emotions are involved, the push to "win at all cost" is invoked, overriding the mission. Once on the track of "win at all cost," we have played into the hands of the person that asked the manipulative question. Turning the competitive argument back into an objective-oriented conversation is difficult.

According to the Word, it is not our mission to win. In Matthew's gospel, Jesus made it clear that the fields are ready for harvest. What was (and is) needed is laborers to the harvest (Matthew 9:37-38). Then, as now, there are fields to harvest that someone else sowed to and cared for, making it clear that there are people that did the work before us (John 4:35-38). In that same manner, we are to do work in which the results will be seen by someone in the future. Remember that many of the saints of old worked tirelessly, never seeing the fruit of that work (Hebrews 11:4-13). Same for us. Our mission is to reconcile mankind to God as made clear in Paul's writing to the church at Corinth (2 Corinthians 5:18-19). We don't get "wins." We simply do our part in the mission, and God collects the "win." Paul also made this clear when he stated that he (Paul) planted, Apollos watered, but the Holy Spirit produced the "win" (1 Corinthians 3:5-6). If we can keep our eyes, our heart, and our head positioned for the mission as Jesus did, then our conversations can be civil.

Point: Know your objective, your mission.

1. You can't save anyone; that is the Holy Spirit's job. There is an old saying, "You can lead a horse to water, but you can't make him drink." The same applies to someone getting saved.

2. You can't convince anyone; that is the Holy Spirit's job. In a civil conversation, you share the truth. You're not trying to convince anyone of anything.

3. Your objective is to reconcile people back to God, not to get them to agree with you or to get them to join your team or your organization.

I believe it was Mark Twain that made the statement, "It's better to remain silent and thought a fool than to speak up and remove all doubt." There's wisdom in that statement, as trying to convince someone that you are right and they are wrong is mostly an exercise in futility. That's one of the reasons Jesus never did that. In fact, He made it clear as He sent His disciples out on their own that if a home or a city did not receive the peace that they spoke over it, for them to retrieve their peace and depart that home or city (Matthew 10:11-14). He did not instruct the disciples to argue the point. By reading their accounts of the journey after returning, we find that they experienced mighty miracles by obeying Jesus. It works the same for us today.

Our job is to position ourselves for the mission. That requires preparation and determination. Fortunately, we have a helper in this, who is not only a helper; He happens to be the mission.

LOVE FROM ABOVE

In our current globalized, tolerant, kumbaya, everything-goes culture today, many people are of the belief that there are no enemies, that everyone should be welcomed with open arms and given anything they want. Then, everyone will be happy, happy, happy. Apparently, Jesus didn't know that. Multiple times in the gospels, He told us to love our enemies (Luke 6:27, 35). (Not *the* enemy, the accuser of the brethren, but our enemies.) Paul taught us in the book of Romans to, as much as is possible, be at peace with everyone (Romans 12:18). Apparently, we are not going to be at peace with everyone. Regardless, we are to love all of them. That is not a simple thing to do.

To love our enemies, we have to first learn what (and who) love is. In our "tolerant" culture, everything in life is wrapped around feelings. Common sense, logic, science, biology, and biblical precepts are all exchanged for how someone feels about things. Feelings and emotions are the cultural drivers, twisting the word "love" to fit that narrow scope.

The hypocritical thing about all of this is that some people who believe that there are no enemies seem to believe that Christians are their enemy. And those same people who have their kind of love for those non-existent enemies seem to have the same amount of hate for Christians. And as much tolerance as they have for those non-existent enemies, they seem to have the same amount of intolerance for Christians. Thus, the origin of the question posed to us in the section on "Offensive Defense," the question that started this entire conversation.

The love that Jesus was talking about is not an emotional love. That love is a choice. It is an action and a behavior. If God is love (and He is), then when we choose God, we choose love (1 John 4:8). That love is a one-sided love. God loves people by choice. He even loves those that don't love Him and those that hate Him. We are to love the same way.

If you love someone (in the manner that you are called to love), then your feelings aren't the driver. Your choice is the driver. How the other person responds to that is not your concern. If you love that person, your job is to tell them the truth. (In His last recorded prayer, Jesus told us that God's Word is truth [John 17:17]). What they do with that truth is between them and God.

Point: Love (agape) the person with whom you are conversing.

1. Love them more than they love themselves. The love they have for themselves is most likely a self-centered love. Your loving them is a God-centered love. By choice is how you love them more than they love themselves.

2. Share that love is more of a who than a what.

3. Show the person that they matter to the Lord and to you.

4. Love the person into reconciliation so that they want what you have.

To love the person more than they love themselves is to care about their eternity. We should seriously want the person to experience a true relationship with God so they won't spend eternity separated from Him. If you truly love the person (in the way Jesus asked us to love them), then we should desire that they spend eternity with us in what we refer to as heaven. That person accepting that path (or not) is not on us. Our job is to share it with them, and sharing that is a much more productive conversation than the argument that our emotions want us to have.

All of this sounds so simple, and most of us agree with it. Putting it to action is a different story. Subtracting our emotions from a face-to-face confrontation is not that easy. It would truly be a wonderful thing if we could just call down the anointing when needed and let the Lord handle it through us. Most of the time, it doesn't work that way, though. God kind of expects us to be participants in the issue. That's why the application of the information in the other sections of this manuscript has to accompany this one. It's a lifestyle more than a practiced art. It's a love from above.

LET'S GET REAL

As you watch a "reality" show, it dawns on you that it's not quite as real as expected. There is something about the little red light on the camera that changes the person being filmed. That is quite understandable, as you and I react somewhat the same way when someone films us. That reaction to the camera is the true reality. Forgetting how to say something, or how you would normally react to someone else saying something while being filmed, changes real.

Public speaking is another function that can have an effect of this nature. The first reaction most people have to a request to speak publicly is to avoid it at all costs. The fear that we have at that point is real, the "butterflies" in your inner being go crazy, and it's difficult to breathe normally. I was in South Africa on a mission trip in the late 1990s when I came face to face with that fear. The man in charge of that mission trip was an awesome, gentle older man with great people skills. He saw something in me that I didn't know I had and, in a gentle manner, pushed me over the edge regularly, only to find (to my surprise) that I possessed the ability to rise to the occasion. On a Sunday morning in a large building being used as a church there in Zimbabwe, with hundreds of people in attendance, he came by where I was standing (attempting to sing with the congregation) and grabbed me by the arm to come with him. He was walking toward the front, the stage. He leaned to my ear and said, "I want you to give your testimony." My heart hit the level of my ankles, and I cannot explain the "butterflies." In my best ability to converse at that point, I questioned when I would be giving that testimony. As we walked up the stairs of the stage, he said, "Right now," and as the music subsided, he handed me a mic. The people in that congregation got to see reality. I did the only thing I knew to do at that point; I asked the Lord for help. He showed up, and I got through that "push over the edge" without embarrassing Him, my mentor, or me, and without making a physical, smelly mess of everything.

In the same manner as that of being filmed or speaking publicly, an argument can pull us away from who we really are. As we've seen in the previous sections, an argument can change a person from being their normal, balanced, caring self into acting like a caged wild animal, trying to prove a point or win the argument. An argument requires adrenalin; a conversation doesn't.

Point: Be real at all times.

1. The person you are talking to may very well believe that you are a hypocrite. Prove that incorrect by your balanced, non-emotional, informative conversation.

2. Your life should be in line with your beliefs and should already be obvious to the person you are talking to prior to the conversation.

3. You have to believe in what you believe in to be believable. It should show to the person with whom you are conversing.

4. If you're talking to darkness, remember that you are the light.

In the twenty-first century, I have spoken publicly many times. In churches, schools, community organizations, and many other public venues. The butterflies are always present prior to speaking; however, I learned something that is worth sharing. We saw in the section "Know Show" that knowing your audience and knowing your subject matter are priorities for public speaking. There is another that needs to be addressed, one that applies equally to public speaking and to having a civil conversation. It's referred to as "anointing," and it is not something that is easily explained. It is not a talking point, rather an experience, an encounter. No matter how someone tries to explain it, the experience of being "under the anointing" changes everything you have heard, and you discover why it is so hard to explain. (The same applies to being saved or being filled with the Spirit.) We have to understand that it is a spiritual thing that affects the physical.

While under the anointing, several things happen that I can never explain:

1. The fear of public speaking disappears.

2. The concern for saying something terribly wrong (e.g., an offensive word) is diminished. The Holy Spirit really doesn't want you to say something that will cause people to miss what He sent you to say.

3. Whatever physical pains you had prior to speaking are gone.

4. Your attention is on what you are called to say, more than what you have in your notes. And if you are truly under the anointing, the Spirit can and sometimes does change the entire presentation while you are speaking.

In the gospel of Matthew, Jesus dispatched the disciples with the disclaimer that the disciples would be treated unfairly and possibly flogged in public for what they were sent to speak. Also, they would be brought before councils to answer for their actions. To that end, Jesus assured them that the Holy Spirit would tell them what they needed to say in those situations (Matthew 10:16-20). That sounds extremely close to what is now referred to as "the anointing." The anointing is real.

By allowing the Spirit to speak through you under the anointing, it becomes apparent to you that the Spirit knows exactly who is in attendance and what each of those people need to hear. There is no way that you or I could know all of that, ergo the need for the anointing. Even without the anointing, though, we should be prepared for what we are speaking, whether speaking publicly or in a conversation. If we continue to study and prepare, the Spirit will assist with that preparation. By keeping the conversation below argument level, that preparation will prove itself correct, allowing for civil discourse and allowing us to be real in our interactions.

In general terms, being real means that you are the same person in all situations. That means that people with whom you completely disagree can be real too. And that's okay, but their being their kind of real should not pull you away from being the real that you were called to be. A good epitaph for a headstone would be, "He was real" (WYSIWYG).

STORY TIME

Everyone loves a good story. That's one of the reasons that story movies have been, and continue to be, so popular. Many of the songs we listen to tell stories in two to three minutes of playtime. Also, many of the books that we read are story-type books. I don't personally know a human being that doesn't enjoy a good story. One of my favorite storytellers of all time was my wife's maternal grandfather. He was what many people refer to today as old school, having grown up in tough times, raising his seven girls and one boy during the depression years. Though I did not know him in his prime, he was obviously a physically strong man with an iron will. (He broke horses for a local ranch until he was fifty-five.) Through all of that, he was one of the most interesting men I've ever met. He rolled his own cigarettes, and the end of his right thumb and index finger were blackened from the years of getting the last pull from the end of each. He had moved to western Texas by the time I met and married my wife, and there were regular trips to go see him and his wife (Granny, we called her. Her real name was Jewel, and she was just that. Had to be to put up with Paw, as we called him). Some of my favorite memories in life were after supper, as Paw would sit out on the front porch and start telling stories. The stories would all start with a respectable amount of truth, but by the end, it was obvious that he was making much of it up as he went. Didn't matter. Sometimes a single story would last for two or three hours.

I am not close to that good at telling stories. You probably aren't either. Doesn't matter. You have a story to tell. Tell it. It's your story; you lived it, you experienced it, and no one can take it from you. Share it during conversation when the time avails itself. Your story can and will impact someone else.

The entire Bible is a story consisting of hundreds of smaller stories that all tie together. It's the most interesting book ever written. The Old Testament is a collection of picture stories (referred to as "types and shadows" by Bible scholars). Tell one of those stories when the opportunity arises. I'm not talking about trying to condemn someone, rather to gain their interest. When you tell a story that someone else thinks they already know in such a way that they see that story completely different when you're done, it can change that person's life.

For example, look at the story of Noah and the flood. Growing up in church, I could never understand why a caring, loving God would destroy almost everyone and everything. (People that don't know or even want to know God are glad to use this story to make their point about the mad, mean God they think they know.) I get that, as I've had my questions about that too. I remember very clearly the morning that my pastor (who knows, understands, and teaches the Word with clarity) shared why God flooded the earth. It's right there in print, but I never got it till then. *All* of the people (except Noah) on earth did *only* evil. God was so patient with mankind that He waited until it was down to one righteous man. Before the world corrupted that man and ruined God's plan for a righteous seed to prevail on earth until His final plan was unveiled (Jesus and the cross), He was forced to protect that seed. That simple explanation of a long-misunderstood Bible story changed my entire process of studying the Bible. If it did that for me, might it not do the same for someone else?

Point: You have a story, a witness, a testimony.

1. It's your story; tell it.

2. It's your experience; no one can dispute it or take it away from you.

3. It changed your life; it could change someone else's.

The last half of the first chapter of Galatians is the story of Paul's journey from Pharisee to Apostle of Christ. He leaves out many details, but by reading it, you get the gist of his conversion and what it cost him. It's an interesting story, and his conversion cost him dearly (Galatians 1:11-24).

When Jesus sent the disciples out to minister in the various towns and villages, He told them straight up that they would meet resistance and that they would be brought before great men. However, He told them not to worry about it because the Spirit would tell them what to say (Matthew 10:19). He will do the same for us today. Our job is to be prepared.

What's your story? Have you told your story? Getting a conversation that can quickly turn into an argument turned so that you and the other person are sharing stories leads to a much more productive conversation. The other side of that coin (so to speak, or as it is put in mathematics, the corollary to that theorem) is this: the person you are conversing (or arguing) with has a story to tell also. Let them tell it. Once they've spoken their piece, you should have your chance to speak. And your story just might make a difference. Every conversation, every day, lends itself to storytime.

TIMING IS IMPORTANT

I was twelve years old when we moved from a residential dwelling in a mid-sized town to the wide-open spaces of a country home. Everything was new to me, including the business that my parents had purchased and were operating while completing their parental duties of raising their rather large family. My dad was an excellent mechanic, and part of the business included a one-stall automotive shop. I came home from school one afternoon to see the insides of an engine laid out neatly on the floor in front of a car, all clean and ready for assembly. I had never seen anything like that before. I had no idea that the engine that so smoothly powered a vehicle down the highway had so many parts and pieces to it! The next day after school, I got to the shop to find that all of those pieces were together and installed in the car. I was just in time to help my dad start that engine. As he leaned over the fender to handle the engine controls, I turned the key to engage the starter, and to my shock (approaching terror), the engine rolled over a couple of times and exploded right in front of my dad's face. In my haste to depart the premises, my feet got tangled in the pedals, and my life began to pass before my eyes. The hood was not on the car, so the flame from the fire was clearly visible through the windshield while I got to witness one of the most courageous acts that I had witnessed to that point in my life. Dad calmly leaned over the engine and blew the flame out as if he were blowing out the candles on a birthday cake. Though he tried to hide it, I could tell that he wanted to laugh out loud at my reaction. I finally got free from the pedals and the door and, with great trepidation, made it to the front of the car with him. As he was wont to do, he took advantage of the moment and taught me something. (I must admit that I was still trembling, and most of his words did not reach their intended destination.)

Through that process and teaching, I learned a valuable lesson that has served me well in my life: timing is important. Dad explained that a gasoline-powered, internal combustion engine has mechanical timing (all of those pieces that were on the floor the day before have to be in time with each other to cause the events that make it run to occur appropriately), and it has to have an electrical spark to invoke the internal combustion (explosion) to occur at the proper time also. In the example above, the electrical timing was off just enough to cause the engine to ignite backward through the carburetor, setting the excess fuel on fire. After he explained what happened, he twisted the distributor and asked me to once again start the engine for him. I trusted my dad, but everything in me was still trying to exit the building. As I turned the key to start the engine this time, it rolled over a few times and started running on its own. A few more adjustments, and the engine purred like a new one. Still teaching, my dad twisted the distributor back and forth to show me how critical timing is to an engine.

Applying that lesson to life, I have found that timing is just as important to my everyday activities, including conversation. Early in life, I learned that some conversations require the correct and appropriate timing. (E.g., while being disciplined for being a disrespectful teenager, it was obvious that it was not the appropriate time for a conversation about my perceived need for the purchase of a car for me to drive to school.) The same can be said about conversations concerning politics. A family gathering for a holiday meal might not be the best setting for contentious political commentary. Many of the people that I have talked with concerning this subject have stated that they are sometimes taken aback by the timing, the setting, or the aggressiveness of this type of conversation and have elected to just remain quiet until a more appropriate time and setting. That would most assuredly be an act of civility. In my study, I found that Jesus, more than once, walked through or past a crowd of people without conversation. And when He did converse, He timed His comments or questions in such a manner that He guided the conversation toward what the other person (or persons) needed to hear.

At the same time, there are also examples of Him removing all conversation and taking complete control of the situation to make the point He was sent to make. In Matthew 21, we find the account of Him removing the moneychangers from the temple, and in Matthew 23, we find Him speaking against the manner in which the Jewish authorities of the day were treating the people. Neither of those examples included conversation; however, in both examples, His timing was exact. There is a difference between conversation and teaching, but both require timing. It is worth mentioning again that it can only be called teaching when someone is learning. Otherwise, it's just talking. And again, conversation requires both speaking and listening by both parties.

When leading (what the corporate world used to refer to as "managing") people, timing becomes even more important, especially when the need for discipline arises. For nearly twenty years of my young adult life, I held a professional position as a department manager for a regional healthcare facility. Most of the people that worked with me in the department also held professional positions. When a project got off course or a personnel issue that needed to be addressed availed itself, I learned early (the hard way) that professional conversation was much preferable to disciplinary action. Most issues could be resolved by allowing the individual time to discuss the issue and give his or her side of the story. In those situations, timing was extremely important. I learned to never, under any circumstance, make an instant judgment or immediately call the person on the issue. Rather, I would spend one, sometimes two nights getting myself settled and prepared for a constructive conversation. Most of the time, that worked without further disciplinary action. (I learned that from my supervisor, the CFO of the organization, whom I hold in the highest regards to this day.)

In today's politically charged atmosphere, the timing of a conversation can certainly allow a person to keep their blood pressure reasonably normal. Sometimes it's best to just let an argument dissipate rather than trying to turn it into a conversation. Another time for the discussion may be more appropriate. God (who lives outside of time) understands timing better than we do. Sometimes our prayers are not answered in what we would see as a timely manner. His timing is always precise, though. We can learn a lot by studying His timing.

EPILOGUE

The eight sections presented are in no way intended to be an exhaustive teaching on civil discourse. Writers with much more wisdom and knowledge than the author of this book could most assuredly provide better guidance and more substance, and there may well be those books already available. It is the intention of this book to simply get the reader to look at conversation from a different perspective and hopefully make some small, positive difference in conversations between Americans.

As I have attempted to apply the sections of this book to my personal conversations, I have found them to be prudent in many cases, and they have helped me on more than one occasion. At the same time, though, I have been unsuccessful at applying them to some conversations. The section on timing applies best in the case of the latter and has made it easier for me to back up from an argument.

More than the information given in this book, though, it is my kingdom walk that drives me in the right direction in conversation. I am committed to that walk, and when my conversation veers from it, conviction pushes me in the same manner that gravity pushes a gyroscope back into balance. As mentioned in the front of this book, I enjoy a good conversation, and it is my hope that I can spend my remaining time on earth in constructive conversation rather than defensive argument.

Paul, at the end of the seventh chapter of the book of Romans, described "fallen man" and the human shortcomings related to that condition. To paraphrase that and apply it to my walk, sometimes I do what I know better than to do, and other times I don't do what I know to do. Same with speaking. Sometimes I say something that I wish I hadn't said or don't say something that I know I should have said. Or worse yet, I say something in a manner that is not constructive or proper, leading to direct push back from the person with whom I am conversing. It is obvious that the ability to have a constructive conversation is in recognizing my defensive posture early and quickly making the adjustments to turn the ensuing argument toward fruitful conversation.

It is also obvious that a book of rules or a checklist is not going to make all of my conversations fruitful. It will take commitment on my part. And more important than my commitment, like everything else in my kingdom walk, it will take help from the Holy Spirit. Jesus knew that too. That's why He sent the Comforter when He left.

Civil Discourse 101

1. Do not allow the other person to put you into a defensive position. They are already prepared to address your defense; you probably aren't:

   A. You do not need to defend your beliefs. They are yours.

   B. You can't defend someone else's beliefs. They have their own.

   C. You don't need to defend the Word. The Word takes care of itself.

   D. You can't defend God. He's either God, or He's not.

2. Ensure that you have a conversation, not an argument:

   A. Remove your emotions from the conversation. Unlike popular opinion states, everything on earth is not about feelings.

   B. Ask questions and listen to the answers.

   C. Wait your turn to speak.

   D. Speak respectfully. Disagree agreeably. The other person has as much right to their belief as you do yours.

   E. Do like Jesus. Disarm them with a question or statement, then share some truth.

3. Know the Word:

   A. Jesus quoted the Word when accosted; we can too.

   B. Understand how the Word applies to life and explain how and why.

C. Bible-thumping will not work! Share from your heart.

D. Share a non-combative story or truth from the Bible. One that will connect with the conversation.

4. Know your objective (mission):

   A. You can't save anyone; that is the Holy Spirit's job.

   B. You can't convince anyone; that is the Holy Spirit's job.

   C. Your objective is to reconcile people back to God, not get them to agree with you or join your team or organization.

5. Love (agape) the person you are conversing with:

   A. Love them more than they love themselves.

   B. Share that love is more who than what.

   C. Show the person that he/she matters to the Lord and to you.

   D. Love the person into reconciliation so they want what you already have.

6. Be *real*:

   A. The person you are talking to may believe that you are a hypocrite. Prove that incorrect with your chaste conversation.

   B. Your life should be in line with your beliefs and should already be obvious to the person with whom you are conversing.

   C. You have to believe in what you believe in to be believable. It should show to the person with whom you are conversing.

D. If you're talking to darkness, remember that you are the light.

7. You have a story, a witness, a testimony:

   A. It's your story; tell it.

   B. It's your experience; no one can dispute it or take it away from you.

   C. It changed your life, and it could change someone else's life. Tell it.

8. Timing is everything:

   A. There's a time and a place for everything, including civil conversation.

   B. An engine out of time runs bad, a conversation out of time ends bad.

   C. God's timing is always correct; maybe we should let God handle the timing.

CPSIA information can be obtained
at www.ICGtesting.com
Printed in the USA
BVHW040242260921
617559BV00005B/18